The Clev

The Clever Potato

Vernon Scannell

Illustrated by Tony Ross

Beaver Books

A Beaver Book
Published by Arrow Books Limited
62-5 Chandos Place, London WC2N 4NW
An imprint of Century Hutchinson Ltd

London Melbourne Sydney Auckland
Johannesburg and agencies throughout the world

First published in 1988 by Hutchinson Children's Books
Beaver edition 1989

Text © Vernon Scannell 1988
Illustrations © Tony Ross 1988

This book is sold subject to the condition that
it shall not, by way of trade or otherwise, be lent,
resold, hired out, or otherwise circulated without the
publisher's prior consent in any form of binding or cover
other than that in which it is published and without a
similar condition including this condition being imposed
on the subsequent purchaser.

Set in Sabon by Rowland Phototypesetting Ltd,
Bury St Edmunds, Suffolk

Made and printed in Great Britain
by The Guernsey Press Co Ltd
Guernsey, C.I.

ISBN 0 09 962280 7

*To Emma Kilcoyne,
a few titbits*

Contents

The clever potato	9
Versatile Murphy	11
Jam roll in custody	13
Grannie's custard pies	14
Eating out of doors	16
Eating out	18
Jelly-lover	20
Sweet mystery	22
Sweet nonsense	24
Sweet song	25
Liquorice Allsorts	26
Meals on wheels	28
Meal times	30
Irish pub grub poem	32
The girl I did not marry	33
Auntie Meg's cookery book	34
The fable of Auntie Mabel	37
The little joke	38
The porcupie	41
The horrible food game	42
The Olympic eating game	44
Sources of sauce	46
Special today	48
Cheese-bored	50
Three snippets	51
Four snacks	52
Mother's milk	52
Poem on bread	54
I bit an apple . . .	55
Food for thought	56
Eating habits	57

The banquet	58
Punishment diet	60
Eyes and stomach	61
Third World hunger	62
The feast	63

Note:
All of these poems were written especially for this book with the exception of 'Poem on bread' and 'I bit an apple . . .', which are reprinted from *The Apple Raid*, long out of print; and 'Special today' which first appeared in the annual *Allsorts*, edited by Ann Thwaite.

The clever potato

Over sixty years ago
A boy of five would walk to school;
Sometimes in the falling snow
Of winter mornings, past the pool,
Frozen white like shrouded glass,
Along Peel's Lane a mile almost
Between pale fields of brittle grass,
Arriving like a little ghost
In Mrs Wiscombe's infant class.

She did not understand why he
Often cried when he got there.
His hands were cold, he said, but she
Did not know that, like a pair
Of coals his fingers burnt, then froze.
She said, 'Tell Mum or Dad to get
Warmer gloves for you than those.'
At home his grannie cried, 'Oh pet,
You should have told us this before!
I've got the very thing for you!'
Next morning Grannie, at the door,
Said, 'Wear your gloves and take this too.
Hold it in both hands, and your
Fingers will not feel the cold.'
And what she handed him was one
Baked potato, firm and gold
From the oven. 'Better run
Or you'll be late,' his grannie said.
'What do I do when I get there?'
He asked.

'You eat it up instead
Of taking lunch for playtime, dear.
You love potatoes. So you see
What clever things potatoes do,
They warm your hands and they can be
A tasty snack. If hungry, you
Can eat your muff!'

    Dear reader, who
Did this story happen to?
And am I sure that it is true?
Well yes, I'm sure because, you see,
The boy who ate his muff was me.

Versatile Murphy

The plain potato, you might think,
Is simple, maybe even dull.
Here's one that I'm about to peel;
It's not unlike a tiny skull

But one without much character;
When peeled and boiled upon your plates
You couldn't really tell him from
His hairless and impassive mates.

Yet wait: this same potato can
Dramatically change its form.
Remember how that little boy
Used to make his cold hands warm?

Just think what can be done with it:
Soft bed for bangers, known as mash;
Roasted golden brown or baked;
With onion and corned beef it's hash.

Chips or what some call French fries
Form a nest for cod or plaice;
They're fine with eggs or on their own –
Or try a hot potato cake.

So many kinds to tempt your tastes;
Small and large, new and old,
Cubic salad, brittle crisps,
Served up either hot or cold.

What's more, potatoes have more names
Than any other veg I know;
Spuds or Murphies, tatties, totties –
All depends on where you go.

And did you know this versatile
Fellow's one you can't confine
To the kitchen's pots and pans?
He can actually make wine!

So let's salute this clever chap,
No matter what his shape or size.
Forget those more exotic plants;
The old potato gets my prize!

Jam roll in custody

They took him to the local nick
    And put him in a cell.
I asked what charge was being brought,
    Although I knew quite well,
For I had handled similar cases
    With logic and with charm:
I specialize in G.G.H. –
    Grievous gastric harm.

My clients have included some
    Very shifty folk:
A ham burglar and shepherd spy,
    A rather half-baked bloke;
A trickster pushing jelly deals
    And lemon soles that trample;
A seafood Highlander, who set
    A rotten Scotch egg sample.

But I, with customary skill,
    Convinced the nodding judge
That Mr Bun, the plaintiff, bore
    All kinds of roll a grudge.
Jam roll was freed and we rejoiced;
    This pastry case was won.
The loser was enraged, of course;
    A very hot cross Bun.

Grannie's custard pies

We do not know what kind of pie
The pieman met by Simon wanted
   Him to buy.
Nor do we know why twenty-four
Singing blackbirds found their way
   Inside one pie.

   Kids' stuff? Perhaps; then tell me why
We call a mix of spuds and mince
   A shepherd's pie.
Why a shepherd? Also why
Call the same dish cottage pie?
   Can you reply?

The missiles thrown by funny men
At each other in old films
   Were custard pies.
I wonder: were they genuine?
Did cooks work hard to keep a flow
   Of fresh supplies?

Or were they fakes; and if they were
What stuff was used to imitate
   Filling and crust?
I guess it wasn't very nice
To judge by those old actors' looks
   Of deep disgust.

If proper custard pies were used
(The kind my grannie used to make)
   They would have queued,
However many thrown at them,
To welcome them with open mouths
   And gratitude.

For grannie's custard pies were so
Utterly delicious, that
   All other pies
In nursery rhymes or bakers' trays,
In competition would not gain
   A single prize.

Sometimes in dreams I see my dear
Grannie working at her stove.
   And when I rise
I smell faint breath of cinnamon,
See yellow filling, golden crust,
   Of Grannie's pies.

Eating out of doors

I'm really not a picnic person;
    what about you?
I never was and never will be;
    and that is true.
In lovely summer weather Mother
    would often say,
'I know! Let's have a picnic, shall we?
    It's a perfect day!'
I never had the heart to tell her
    I'd rather stay
Indoors at home and read a comic
    or go out to play.
Anything in fact was better
    than all those flies
Settling on the jam and butter;
    sand in your eyes
Or gritty in your fish-paste sandwich
    while you sit
On cow pat or on wicked thistles –
    I *hated* it!
And wasps like little fighter-bombers
    zooming down
To plant their stings, or in your orange juice
    suicidally drown.
I could have done without all that,
    and still can.
Do I make myself quite clear? I'm not
    a picnic man.
In fact one of the few advantages
    in growing up

Is you can always take your meals at table
    from plate and cup.
And if some well-meaning idiot decides
    with a smile to invite
You to a meal on the sand or grass
    when the sun is bright,
You can firmly say, 'No thanks', or something
    not quite so polite.

Eating out

Waiters glide on castors;
They are black and white
As nuns or priests or pastors,
And tremendously polite.

The wine gleams in the glasses
Like rubies or melted sun;
Here are the Upper Classes
Feeding and having fun.

They nibble at caviare,
Lobster and crêpe suzette;
Then for him a big cigar
And for her a cigarette.

As he sips coffee and brandy
Not caring about the price,
She wishes that pastry and candy
Were not so temptingly nice.

At the other end of town
Sit Elsie Cotter and Stan,
In the café next door to 'The Crown'
Where their evening began.

'The usual, dear?' Stan says.
Then: 'Sausage and chips if you please –
We never change our ways –
Four slices and two teas!'

'Be there in a couple of minutes,'
Says the owner, Charlie Phipps;
And shouts down to his missis,
'Send up two sausage and chips!'

And he pours the tea and smears
A rumour of marg on the bread.
This couple have come here for years,
Ever since they first got wed.

They don't want fancy grub
With all those foreign spices,
But they love a night in the pub,
Then bangers, chips and four slices.

Jelly-lover

Jill likes stuff that wobbles, quivers,
Trembles and gives little shivers,
Ripples, promising rich pleasure,
Glitters like Aladdin's treasure,
Green or red or orange, yellow,
Sharp and fruity, sweet and mellow.
Jill likes jelly in her belly,
She would eat it from a welly;
Loves to see it shake and shudder,
Brightly joggle, jounce and judder.
She adores its slippery motion
And could wallow in an ocean,
Not of green and foamy briny
But lime jelly, smooth and shiny.
Jill, whose best friend calls her Jilly,
Said, 'I hope I don't sound silly
If I say my dream vacation
Has to be an invitation
To an island, gold and shining,
Where I'd spend all day reclining
By a sprinkling sherbet fountain
Shaded by a jelly mountain.'

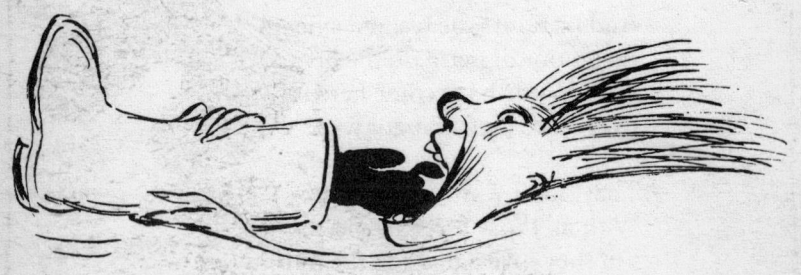

Sweet mystery

When I was young, say nine or ten,
I wondered how grown-ups could bite
On just one chocolate and then
Put all the others out of sight.

I'm sure you've seen them do it, too:
A whole great double-layered box;
And what does Dad and Mother do?
They'll take just one from all those chocs.

The same with any kind of sweets —
Toffees, wine gums, all that stuff —
The most a grown-up ever eats
Is one or two, and that's enough.

When young, I could not comprehend
Why they resisted that sweet treasure.
I thought they must be round the bend,
Refusing unrestricted pleasure.

Not for the life of me, could I
Understand why adults who
Had loads of money did not buy
Tons of gorgeous stuff to chew.

And now that I am old and grey,
And rather fat, I'll tell you what:
I *still* can't understand why they,
Once started, never ate the lot.

Sweet nonsense

The power that made the lolly pop
Could also make the acid drop.
And, if they do, don't be afraid
To go in search of lemon aid.
And if you see the chocolate flake
Patch it with a Pontefract cake
But boil this first in a marzi pan.
So be a smarty girl or man,
And you'll be asked to Sweetmeat Hall
To dance all night at the aniseed ball.

Sweet song
For Nancy and Jane

This is the sweet song,
Song of all the sweets,
Caramel and butterscotch,
Bulls-eyes, raspberry treats;

Treacle toffee, acid drops,
Pastilles, crystal fruits,
Bubble gum and liquorice sticks
As black as new gumboots;

Peppermint creams and aniseed balls,
Tiny sweets and whoppers,
Dolly mixtures, chocolate drops,
Gigantic gobstoppers;

Lemon sherbets, jelly babies,
Chocolate cream and flake,
Nougat, fudge, and sweets that give
You tooth and belly ache.

But the sweets I end my song with
Could never give me pain
In tooth or tummy – anywhere.
One's Nancy; one is Jane.

Liquorice Allsorts

i

Shiny, solid, black
cylinder; tiny topper;
hat without a brim.

ii

Little round cushion
wholly covered by hundreds
of purple pinheads.

iii

Small black length of hose
totally filled with close-packed
perfectly smooth snow.

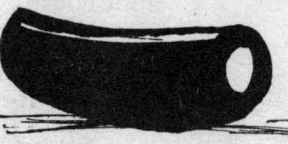

iv

Cubic sandwiches,
white or coloured, with fillings
like black postage stamps.

v

A coconut ruff;
thick wheel of pink or yellow
with ebony hub.

vi

Mix all together;
a treasury of flavours;
bitter-sweet colours.

Meals on wheels

Bombing down the motorway
Doing ninety miles an hour
From a Chinese takeaway
Roared a dish of sweet-and-sour.

Going the other way went past
A slower meal on wheels, a platter
Carrying a simply vast
Quantity of cod in batter.

While down a quiet country lane,
Slow and gentle on two wheels
Cycling on in sun and rain
Rode a bowl of jellied eels.

Next purred the almost silent voice
Coming from a shining car
Made by Messrs. Rolls and Royce,
Full of Russian caviare.

And finally the great dray horse
Hauled on wheels of steel and wood
Triumphantly our favourite course:
Roast beef and veg and Yorkshire pud.

Meal times

Breakfast is the only meal
Whose name we all agree upon;
No other fancy names for this,
It's called the same by everyone.

Not so the other meals we eat:
When I was small I used to take
To school a sandwich or a bun
To eat during the playtime break.

We always used to call this 'lunch'
And what they now call 'lunch' was 'dinner'.
If you name noon as 'dinner time'
You're treated like a fool or sinner.

Some really snobbish or perhaps
Just old-fashioned folk are heard
Saying 'luncheon'. Would they call
My noon chip butty by that word?

I doubt it. Now, what's right for 'tea'?
Thin bread and butter and one cake?
Maybe, but first I'd get stuck in
To chips and sausages or steak.

'Dinner' time's been moved to evening
By members of the Upper Classes;
They swallow soup and meat and pudding,
Swigging wine from gleaming glasses.

It all depends on where your home is:
South or North; what kind of street.
Wise folk don't worry what the meal's called;
They just thank God that they can eat.

Irish pub grub poem

Inside a Galway inn one night,
Resting after walking miles,
I asked the landlord if I might
See the menu. He, with smiles,
Held a piece of paper out

So far off I couldn't read it.
Then he said, 'You do not need it.
Each day we have the same old grub –
Why read the menu in this pub?'

The girl I did not marry

When I was eighteen years of age
   I met a lovely girl;
She was so beautiful she made
   My thoughts and senses whirl.

Not only beautiful but kind,
   Intelligent as well;
Her smile was warm as India,
   Her voice, a silver bell.

So gentle and so sensitive,
   She was the one for me;
We loved the same great melodies
   And peace and poetry.

In spring we wandered hand in hand
   Towards a treasured scene
To which I'd never taken her,
   Small paradise of green.

We climbed a gentle slope and then
   Walked through a little wood;
And there, below, were shining fields
   Where sheep and young lambs stood

Or danced or drifted on dry seas,
   Their bleatings frail or hoarse.
'When I see those,' my darling said,
   'I always smell mint sauce.'

Auntie Meg's cookery book

Tom liked his Auntie Meg a lot,
    But even he confessed
She could not cook at all although
    She *thought* she was the best.

She was a sport. She did not pry
    Or lecture Tom or nag;
He loved to go and stay with her
    Except for that big snag:

She was the worst cook in the world
    And *thought* she was the best;
When she spent hours preparing cakes
    He had to act impressed.

But worse, he had to *eat* the things;
    Her rock cakes were no joke;
Not quite as hard as rock perhaps,
    More like well-seasoned oak.

She often made a dumpling stew.
    Today, Tom still recalls
Those dreaded objects in the pot
    Like little cannonballs.

Her rice was gritty, porridge burnt;
    You could have used her steak
For soling shoes, and one dropped bun
    Once made the whole house shake.

The only way to dodge those meals
 Was find some other craze
So interesting it would take up
 All of her waking days.

So Tom persuaded her to write
   A book. 'What kind?' she said.
'About what most appeals to you,
   Pleasing heart and head.'

'A cookery book!' she cried. 'Oh yes!'
   As lively as a kitten.
'Dear Tom I'll write the very best
   That anyone has written.'

And that's exactly what she did,
   Scribbling day and night.
They had their meals in restaurants
   To Tom's concealed delight.

At last her masterpiece appeared,
   And she at once became
An expert in the cooking arts
   With quickly spreading fame.

A star of radio and screen
   Was dear old Auntie Meg,
And only Tom, her nephew, knew
   She couldn't boil an egg.

The fable of Auntie Mabel

Absent-minded Auntie Mabel
Got so drunk she was unable
To crawl out from beneath the table:
Most unlike dear Auntie Mabel!

We found out later that this awful
Scene occurred because forgetful
Mabel suffered such a woeful
Lapse of memory, almost fatal.

She forgot to put the trifle
In her favourite sherry trifle:
So this is what we like to label
Mabel's sherry-trifle fable.

The little joke

Grown-ups insist on picking on
    Their children all the time.
I'm sure you must have noticed this;
    I reckon it's a crime.

'Do that. Do this. And don't do that.
    Eat up your cabbage. Yes,
Of course you must eat everything.
    And don't make such a mess!'

They make you swallow nasty things
    But when it comes to stuff
Like chocolate or liquorice
    They say, 'You've had enough!

Don't be so greedy. Wrap it up!
    Save it! Make it last!
You greedy little horror don't
    Gobble it so fast!'

They like to call you greedy, these
    Nagging grown-ups do.
But let me tell you something now:
    They're just as bad as you.

Of course their tastes are different from
    The things that you enjoy,
But they will fill themselves as full
    As any girl or boy.

Cigars replace the chocolate bars,
  Wine or whiskey, Coke.
But the greed's the same as any child's,
  That's the little joke.

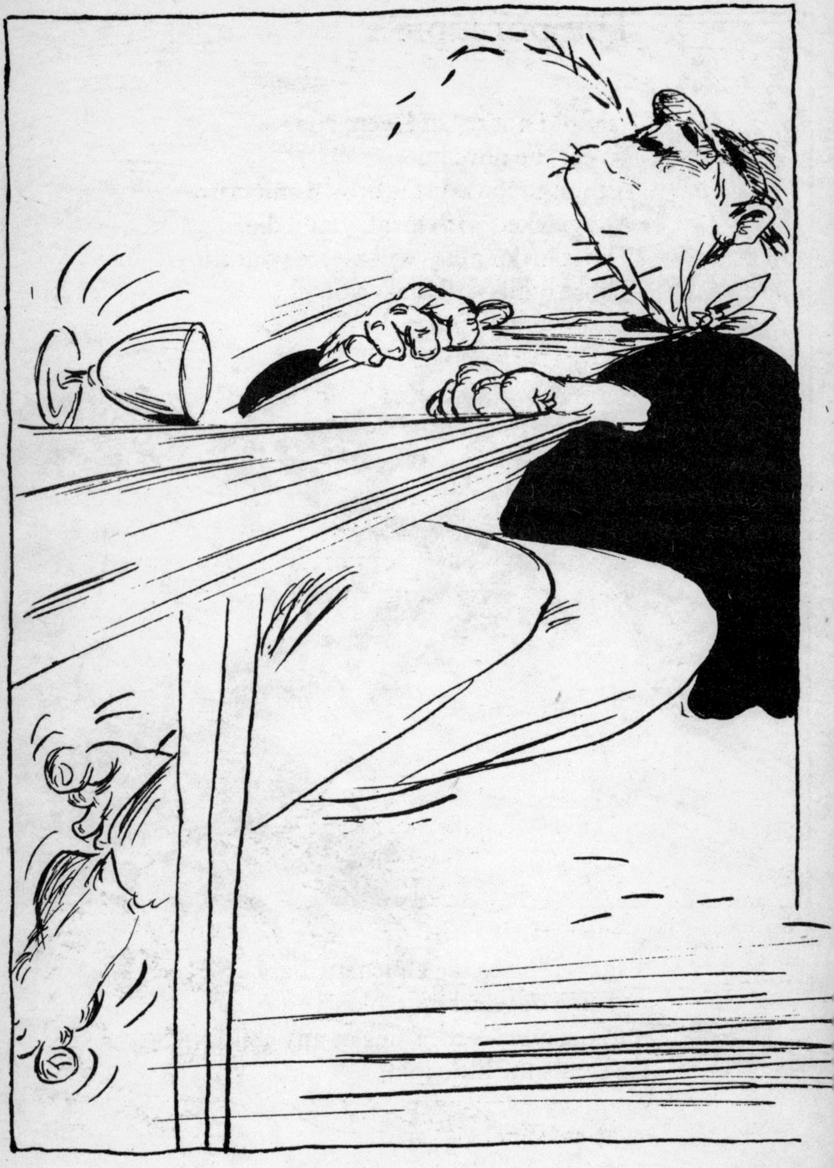

The porcupie

I should not try, if I were you,
To eat the porcupie;
Although the crust is brown and crisp
And packed with meat, you'll die.
Those little spikes will pierce your throat,
Those quills will make you ill,
And you will find no antidote,
No medicine or pill.
So let the little porcupie
Go quietly to its lair
And satisfy your appetite
With apple, plum or pear;
So porcupies may occupy
A world made safe for porcupies
Here and everywhere.

The horrible food game

Here's a game that you can play
To pass a dreary rainy day:
It might be more fun with a friend
But if you find you have to spend
A few hours on your own, why not
Play it solo? It's a lot
More fun than afternoon TV.
All you have to do is think
Of loathsome meals that really stink,
And write a menu which you fill
With dishes guaranteed to kill
Not only appetite but who
Might be mad enough to chew
The awful grub dreamt up by you.
Of course you've no need to include
Any ordinary food
However nasty; what you must
Try to do is put your trust
In pure imagination's powers
To make vile weeds as well as flowers.

A brief suggestion for first course —
Boiled worms in chalk-and-treacle sauce,
Followed by raw donkey steak
Or choice of baked and garnished snake
With toenail cuttings lightly grilled,
And for your sweet a pudding filled
With liquid soap and Vaseline
Served with rancid margarine.
You see the kind of thing I mean?

Okay, get on with it and try
To sicken and to horrify
A friend or, better, enemy.
But – please – whoever it may be
Don't show your nightmare meals to me!

The Olympic eating game

My dear old schoolfriend, Pendleby Reid,
Could eat up his grub at incredible speed;
Savoury, sweet, seasoned and sour,
All disappeared in well under the hour.
He could eat all the day and all the night too,
You wouldn't believe what that man could get
    through.
So when the Olympic Committee's report
Announced that the Games would include a new
    sport,
A race to find out who could swallow the most –
Believe it or not – mud pies and burnt toast,
Who was the Briton most sure to succeed?
The champion of chomping old Pendleby Reid!
The contest took place in the great Eating Ring
And everyone cheered and started to sing
As Pendleby swallowed his toast and mud pies
With speed and with relish, amazing all eyes.
His rivals surrendered, all except one,
The Chinese competitor, Choo Ing Flan Phun.
At last it seemed certain that Pendleby must
Defeat Choo Ing Flan, who looked certain to
    bust.
But then to the horror of Pendleby's faction
He suddenly lost his smooth-eating action
And flung down his shovel-sized spoon with a
    cry,
'I cannot go on, there's a hair in my pie!'
He lost by a whisker, and my story's told
Of how my friend Pendleby failed to win Gold.

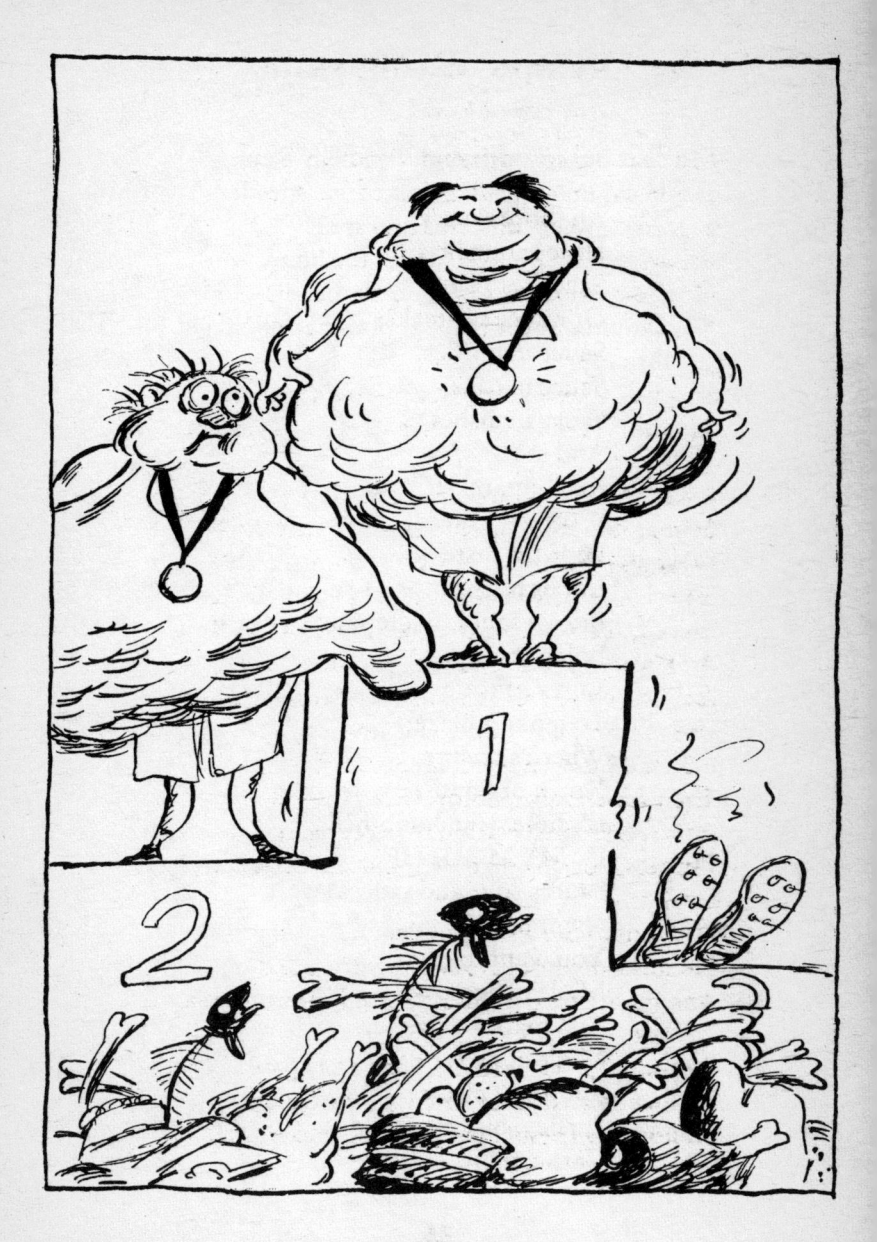
1
2

Sources of sauce

*A rap poem to be read
aloud very quickly
and with a saucy expression.*

All those sauces,
Different makes;
Sauce for fish
Or mince or steaks;
Sauce in bottles,
Sauce in cans,
Sauce in dishes
And in pans;
Ketchup, relish,
Worcester sauce,
Hide the taste of
Cat or horse;
Brown sauce, white sauce,
Bolognese,
Curry sauce
To make a blaze;
Where's the fire,
North or South?
It's here, you dumb-bell,
IN MY MOUTH!
Sauces sour and sauces sweet
On anything
You want to eat;
Made of eggs
And made of cheese,
Made of any-
thing you please;
Parsley, butter,
Garlic, mint,

Sage and pepper,
Just a hint
Of fiery chilli
Whose dry flame
Contradicts
Its icy name;
Onion sauce and
Tasty tartar,
Oyster sauce
And bright tomato.
(I know 'tomato'
Doesn't rhyme
Quite with 'tartar',
I hadn't time
To hunt around
To find some smarter
Chiming words
Like 'Magna Carta'.)
Of all those sauces
We can choose
What's the sauce
We can't refuse?
Not fancy stuff
But this of course:
The family favourite,
Daddy's Sauce!
Who says so? I do,
Saucy lad –
The sauce provider,
Your old Dad.

Special today

i

We can recommend our soups
   And offer thick or thin.
One is known as 'Packet',
   The other known as 'Tin'.

ii

The flying fish makes a very fine dish;
   As good as plaice or skate
When sizzled in fat; but be certain that
   You tether it to your plate.

iii

Now this hot dog makes an excellent snack;
   Our sausages are best pork.
If you can't get it down, please don't send it back,
   Take it for a nice brisk walk.

iv

Are you tempted by our fried fish fingers?
    The last customer to succumb
Was hard to please; he demanded
    Why we couldn't provide a fish thumb.

v

Bubble and squeak is splendid stuff,
    And Chef takes endless trouble.
But if you feel you'd like a change
    Then try our squeak and bubble.

vi

If you choose our historical steak
    You'll chew and chew and chew
And know what Joan of Arc,
    When tied to one, went through.

vii

You may have tried most kinds of pie
    But have you ever dared
To munch a circular portion of
    Crusty πr^2?

viii

Try our cabinet pudding
    Or a slice of home-made cake;
We serve with each, quite free of charge,
    A pill for your belly ache.

Cheese-bored

Wensleydale and Rocquefort,
  Gruyère, Danish blue,
Rubbery Dutch and Camembert,
  And out go you.

Cheddar, Cheshire, Stilton,
  Gorgonzola, Brie,
Caerphilly, Parmesan,
  And out goes me.

Three snippets

i

The strawberry cried,
'I'm in a jam!
I don't know why
But here I am.'

Said Roly-poly,
'So I see.
I know because
The jam's in me.'

And Tubby Tibbs,
The greedy lad,
Devouring both
Said, 'Just too bad!'

ii

Jack and the beans talk
About the kind of thing
That you and I would not discuss
With a cabbage or a king.

iii

Old Mother Hubbard
Sat in the cupboard
Eating Jack's Christmas pie;
He opened the door,
Gave a furious roar
And blacked Mother Hubbard's right eye.

Four snacks

i

Ebony bracelets,
Linked like plump Siamese
　twins:
Coal heavers' handcuffs.

ii

A crusty brown purse
Without a zip, it contains
Savoury riches.

iii

Elongated worms,
White entrails steaming in
　blood:
Grub for the hangman.

iv

Yellow shining disc,
Morning sun on soft white sky:
A toast is proposed.

Mother's milk

Shortly after John began
To go to school his brother Jake,
Two years older, said to John
During Monday morning break:
'Guess what! I've got amazing news!
When you go home to have your tea
You'll find a stranger in the house.
I promise you! Just wait and see!'

So after school, John hurried home
To see what Jake was on about;
And what he found astonished him
So much he gave a squeaky shout
And then he yelled, 'Oh Mum! What's that?'

'Not *what* is that but *who*,' she smiled,
And looked down where, upon her lap,
She nursed a tiny newborn child.

'This is Toby,' Mother said.
'You've got another brother, dear!'
John thought at first that he would like
To see the creature disappear.
But very soon his feelings changed;
He found he liked the babe instead
Of feeling jealous, and he loved
To watch him bathed and changed and fed.

A few weeks later, John came home
After school and said, 'Today
We were told that cows eat grass,
And grass turns into milk. But hey!
What I want to know is this –'
He frowned with puzzled eyes at Mother –
'I've never seen you eating grass,
How come you've milk to feed my brother?'

Poem on bread

The poet is about to write a poem;
He does not use a pencil or a pen.
He dips his long thin finger into jam,
Or something savoury preferred by men.
This poet does not choose to write on paper;
He takes a single slice of well-baked bread
And with his jam or Marmite-nibbed forefinger
He writes his verses down on that instead.
His poem is fairly short as all the best are.
When he has finished it he hopes that you
Or someone else – your brother, friend or sister –
Will read and find it marvellous and true.
If you can't read, then eat: it tastes quite good.
If you do neither, all that I can say
Is he who needs no poetry or bread
Is really in a devilish bad way.

I bit an apple . . .

I bit an apple and the flesh was sweet:
Juice tingled on the tongue and from the fruit
Arose a scent that memory received
And in a flash raised ghosts of apple trees,
Leaves blistered with minutest bulbs of rain
Bewildering an autumn drawing room
Where carpets stained with unaccustomed
    shadow
Heard one old table creak, perhaps moved too
By some remembrance of a former time
When summer, like a lover, came to him
And laid amazing offerings at his feet.
I bit an apple and the spell was sweet.

Food for thought

To choose your food and drink with care is wise,
It keeps the body healthy. But beware –
The mind deprived of goodness ails and dies.

Look out for mental junk food, sugared lies
Published on the page or on the air;
To choose your food and drink with care is wise.

The rubber sausages and cardboard pies
Are filled with rubbish, quite atrocious fare;
The mind deprived of goodness ails and dies.

So when you need to feed the brain and eyes,
Don't settle for what happens to be there;
To choose your food and drink with care is wise.

The frozen sawdust burger and French fries
Make flabbiness increase; I also swear
The mind deprived of goodness ails and dies.

Don't be deceived by what they advertise,
And take to heart those wise words which
    declare
To choose your food and drink with care is wise;
The mind deprived of goodness ails and dies.

Eating habits

The whole world is a busy eating house:
The poor eat what the rich might give their dogs,
The squire scoffs salmon, caviare and grouse,
Italians feed on pasta, French on frogs;
Flowers and trees devour the sun and rain,
The ocean nibbles rocks, cows chomp on grass,
The evil weevil eats the farmer's grain;
Not only Asians relish meat Madras;
Cats munch on mice and fish eat other fish,
Flies eat up muck and bugs drink human blood,
Parsons are the cannibals' favourite dish,
And earthworms love a banquet of rich mud;
While Time, the huge moth none of us can see,
Eats everything, including you and me.

The banquet

Two hundred guests have come to see who wins
The prize; two hundred guests, four hundred
    chins,
The fattest and the richest in the land
Assembled at their tables in this grand
Hall where banquets such as this occur
For those whose wives come dressed in costly fur,
And diamonds of course. The prize is for
The businessman who's managed to make more
Profits than the rest of them this year.
It's won by merchant banker, Hugh de Vere.
Smoked salmon, caviare and stuff like that
Is rapidly converted into fat.
Wine is poured and pompous speeches made
To cheers when workers are called 'overpaid'.

Behind the scenes where work is being done
Alphonse, the master chef, has now begun
His ritual inspection of the meat
As it emerges from the oven's heat
And, sizzling, stands before his expert gaze.
He pauses for a moment, to appraise
The texture of those fragrant juicy joints
And, when he has approved them, he appoints
Various assistants to their posts
To work at their dissection of the roasts.
Alphonse himself prepares the joint to please
The pampered palates of the VIPs.
He brandishes his knife, prepares to carve
While yet another million children starve.

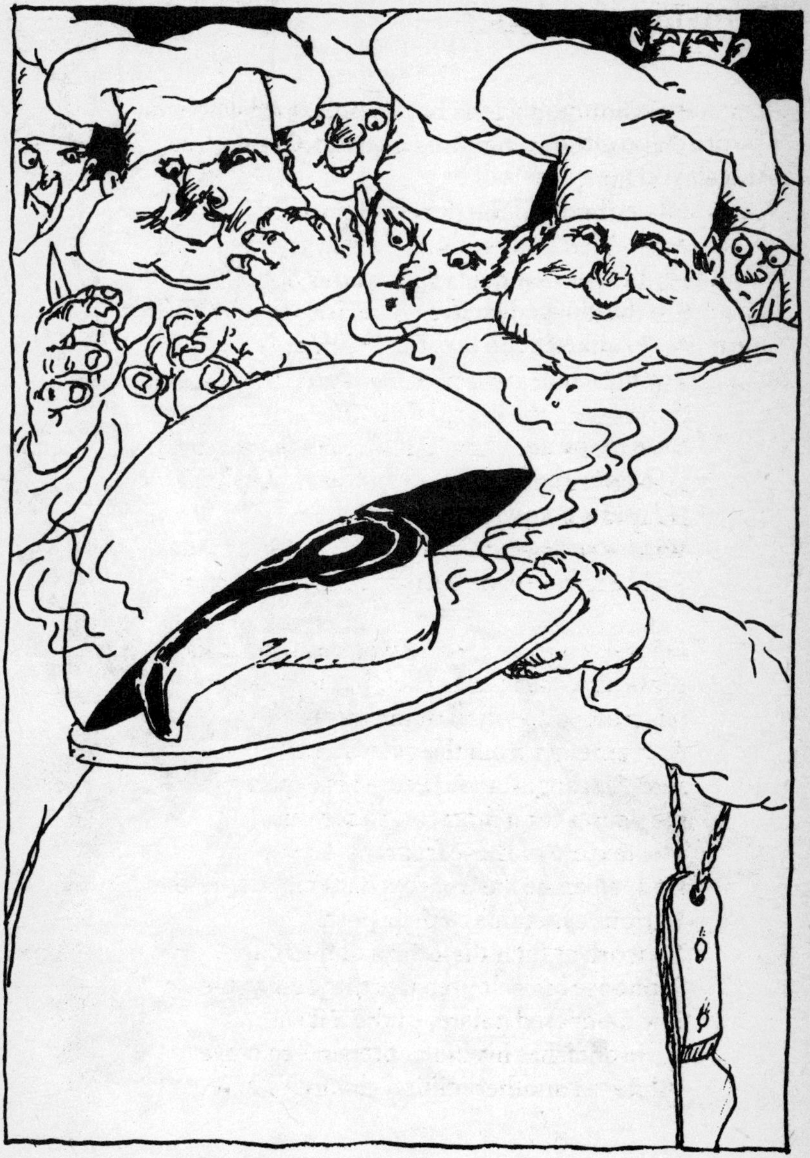

Punishment diet

'A solitary cell for you,'
The prison governor said,
'And all you get to eat will be
Water and dry bread.'

Thousands of miles away,
In a cruelly sun-flogged land,
One more shrunken child lay still
In unprotesting sand.

A child quite innocent,
Harmless to man and beast;
That bread and water would have been,
To him, a glorious feast.

Eyes and stomach

When, as a child, I asked for more –
Not hungry like poor Oliver Twist,
But simply greedy – Grannie swore
That I should learn how to resist
Temptation to eat up too much.
'Your eyes,' she always said, 'are bigger
Than your stomach.' She would touch
Her own eyes and her ample figure,
Smiling gently. I recall
Her words as now, so many years
Later on, I see this small
And solemn child through splintered tears;
This little African with eyes
Big indeed, but not beside
That pathetic belly's size,
Huge as pain and genocide;
Each eye, dark signal of distress,
The belly vast with emptiness.

Third World hunger

Two thousand years ago Christ fed
    the multitude,
In loaves and little fishes found
    a plenitude.
Though we're well fed we hunger still
    and need His word,
As those forsaken continents
    we call the Third
World now starve for love and bread.
    Its peoples' calls
For mercy and deliverance
    should appal
The fat disciples who make gestures,
    that is all;
And from the bitter skies the tears
    of Christ still fall.

The feast

'Feed my lambs' St John XXI v.15

The child was lost in a dark place
Of angry winds and bitter rain;
Icy needles bruised his face,
His feet walked on cold stones of pain.

Thirst and hunger lit black fires,
Whose frozen petals burst inside
His weary body like desires
That never could be satisfied.

And then he met a stranger who
Took him by the hand and said,
'Come with me my child and you
Will find warm shelter and be fed

Here in the cottage of the Lord.'
The child went in with lighter tread
And saw, set out on well-scrubbed board,
Two lighted candles, wine, and bread.